ALABASTER

Scripture quotations taken from The Holy Bible, New International Version® NIV®
Copyright © 1973 1978 1984 2011 by Biblica, Inc. TM
Used by permission. All rights reserved worldwide.

Library of Congress Cataloging-in-Publication Data is available upon request.
Library of Congress Control Number: 2019904353

ISBN: 978-1-7337693-2-7

Contact:
hello@alabasterco.com
www.alabasterco.com

Alabaster Co explores the intersection of creativity, beauty, and faith. Founded
in 2016. Founded in Los Angeles.

All That Is Made

CONTENTS

FOREWORD

In many ways, *All That Is Made* began with Alabaster. It was dreamed about in warehouse coffee shops across Los Angeles and grew up over the first two years of Alabaster's life as a company. It reflects the progression of our creative approach, spiritual thinking, and artistic growth. The pages you hold contain elements of all that we have made until now.

This book is a line of inquiry, a way of questioning and exploring life at the intersection of faith and creativity. The ideas and meditations that we offer are not answers but launching points into deeper thinking on spiritual living and creative practice. We want to offer readers hope, healing, and possibility.

...

All That Is Made is both a theological reflection and an invitation. Blending these elements brings forward a conversation that is both contemplative and active.

First, we believe in a Creator who has created all that is made. We live, breathe, move, and die within this created reality. Our making is always held against the canvas of a larger making at the hands of the God who loves.

As humans, we are invited by God to create within the world of made things. We participate in all that is made through our creating.

We hope that this book is not an ending, but a beginning. That it inspires, comforts, and launches you into a new kind of making. Blessings on the journey.

Geoff Gentry and Bryan Ye-Chung

Part One

A Liturgy for Creatives

01 / What Is Liturgy?

You may have noticed an increase in the use of the word liturgy across the Christian landscape in the last few years. From books, to podcasts, to churches, to sermons, to everyday conversation—Christians are talking about liturgy. But what does it mean when we talk about liturgy in the context of a life with God?

Derived from the Greek word, *leitourgia*, liturgy translates directly to "work of the people." Liturgy is our public work of faith. Practically, this tends to look like ordered, structured prayers and statements of faith read together in the context of a community or church.

But what do we mean when we talk about a liturgy for creatives? We hope the reflections and prayers that follow in these pages will serve as a springboard for deeper theological thinking and spiritual reflection about the role of creatives in the flourishing of humanity.

Structurally, these pages provide a brief introduction to key concepts for Christian creatives to think through and offers prayers to be read aloud (as noted by the italics at the end of each chapter).

We hope this will guide you in shaping a compelling public faith for your creative life and provide a framework for participating in the creative "work of the people." Our dream is that this section gives voice to things you've felt while casting vision for what could be.

02 / Silence

It is hard to live on the Earth in the 21st century and not be painfully aware that life is full of noise. We bounce from notifications, to social media timelines, to advertisements, to endless entertainment options. Most of us love it. Conversation is constant. We live distracted lives, turning our days into content that we fire into the world at an alarming rate. This hurried and marginless living is undergirded by the anxiety of always being "on."

The ability to sit, without a phone or some other device engaging us, has largely been lost. But the art of staying in silence is a crucial rhythm for living lives of deeply rooted faith.

In silence, our soul is quieted. Our burdens—the things we carry, can rise to the surface. Our pain and suffering can be named. Our chaos can be calmed. Our lives can settle in the presence of God's Spirit.

Silence is for calming, for emptying out, for letting go. In silence, we allow Jesus to do his work.

This quieting creates a vital context for creating. Practices of silence, of disconnecting, of letting our mind empty ultimately sustain our creating over the long arc of our lives.

When we create from a place of panic, overload, and anxiety, we are not

allowing ourselves to create from the deep stream of life that Jesus creates from. Creating from a place of overload and stress is like trying to live life in an all-out sprint; eventually your body will give out.

Our invitation is to practice silence, to let the muddy water of our soul settle, and from that place of quiet start the work of creating.

Father, we come to you burdened by the noise and struggles of our world. The demands of living weigh heavy, and our work often feels like toil.

Jesus, quiet the anxious cadence of our hearts. We offer our burdens to you: our unresolved suffering, our confusion, our places of stuckness. We disconnect from our connected living to connect with you.

Holy Spirit, teach us to find your presence in stillness. In silence, help us find refreshment. We welcome the gentle teacher that is a quieted soul. Let our work of creating come from deep reservoirs of peace. Amen.

03 / Imagining Another Reality

The call of the creative is the call to imagine another reality. Whether it is by shedding light on the ways in which our current living falls short of God's vision for humanity, or by articulating the possibilities of a shalom here on earth—the creative ultimately helps us locate ourselves within the larger story of God's unfolding work in all of creation.

Creatives rearrange the materials of the Earth to tell old stories in fresh ways. In Christianity, it is our creative peoples that keep a finger on the pulse of the Spirit.

It is our artists, our poets, and our entrepreneurs who remind us that how it is right now, is not how it will always be. It is creatives that remind us that the arc of the universe bends towards God's justice. It is creatives that both give voice to our suffering and imagine a world in which it is not wasted.

Our invitation now is to join Jesus in imagining another reality.

Jesus, help us see the new thing that is just below the surface. Show us the new creating that you have for us today. May the things we make help others feel known and alive.

Father, give us your perspective on our human condition. Remind us of the dignity in all peoples. Name the false narratives that we struggle with. Give us the courage to make something honest.

Holy Spirit, guard our hearts from despair as we name true things about human suffering. Ground our mind in the suffering of others as we name the true things of hope. Let us imagine with the mind of Christ. Amen.

04 / The Invitation to Innovate

The creative process is not static. We are invited to try new things, to iterate and innovate. The life of creating is the life of continuous iterations—co-creating with Jesus and somehow finding an abundance of life in that process.

In Western Christian communities, there is often subtle (or not-so-subtle) pressure to have a clear and unchanging plan for how life will be lived. Get a degree, get a job, get married, have kids, buy a house, and on and on and on. These are not bad things, but this linear way of living often grates against the artist's soul. For people who gravitate towards mystery, the idea of life without wandering doesn't quite sound like life at all!

Fortunately, there is space in the life of following Jesus for innovation. In our creating, there is room to try new things. There is room to not know.

Life unfolds, and we can iterate and innovate on our way to something abundant and fruitful.

Holy Spirit, lead us as we try on different ways of living within our life. Give us peace of mind as we innovate, iterate, and try new things. Give us joy in our wondering about life.

Jesus, however we innovate, may it be on your path. Keep us grounded in your grace, and teach us to innovate in ways that bless the people around us.

Father, would we feel your pleasure as we wrestle with the lives within our life. Remind us of your love, and keep us humble in the exhilaration of exploration. Amen.

05 / The Creative's Role in God's Invisible Kingdom

As creative people, we are invited to help usher in God's invisible kingdom. This is sacred and meaningful work, but it is always happening at the intersection of perception and invisibility. In Luke 17, Jesus speaks to other religious teachers about what the Kingdom of God looks like. He mysteriously states that the Kingdom can't be detected by visible signs—that people looking with ordinary eyes won't be able to say, "Here it is," or "It's over there."

And then Jesus states, "the kingdom of God is in your midst."

God's presence: invisible, yet embodied.

Jesus was talking about a Kingdom that can't be seen, touched, or detected by visible signs. God was ushering in his invisible Kingdom by placing his Spirit into the heart of humanity.

By default, humans want something palpable, material, and concrete. We want to experience something real, something we can explain with our senses. Think about the Israelites—as soon as their physical connection to God (in the person of Moses) disappeared on Sinai, their faith wavered and they turned to a golden calf. They wanted a god they could see and touch. Their God-ordained purpose was misdirected, and the result was their making something that was beautiful but lifeless.

What can we learn as creatives? We are called to bring the invisible, intangible qualities and attributes of the

Kingdom into this visible world. We are called to purposefully create by the divine Spirit of God.

When Moses came down the mountain with instructions for the tabernacle, the altar, and the priestly garments, he was bringing not-yet-realized elements of God's rule and reign into the community. It required the Israelites to go to work. They redirected their skill, focus, and energy into creating something that would ultimately be filled with the living presence of God.

When we embody the attributes of God's kingdom, our work—our acts of creating—are infused with those qualities. Love. Joy. Peace. Heaven, on earth.

Creatives render the invisible qualities of God visible in real space and time. As Kahlil Gibran states, "Work is love made visible."1 This makes all the difference when working in God's kingdom. Our making is an outward expression of the internal work of God's life-giving breath in us.

The physical manifestation of God's Spirit in you, and his kingdom residing in you, is not only a changed heart but a changed environment. Wherever you go, there is the Kingdom. And whatever you create, there is an invisible quality to it that draws people deeper into God's presence.

You have a part—let that sink in. Everything you create in the Spirit of the One who gives purpose is another building block in his glorious work to bring his peace, wholeness, love, and light to this world.

Jesus, remind us of the truth that your kingdom is already among us. You invite us to work alongside you, and we are grateful for the invitation.

Father, keep our hands focused on the work that you have called us to. Keep us from distraction, and grow the fruits of the Spirit in our working lives.

Holy Spirit, work through us to reflect the qualities and character of God into the things that we make. Let our work become like love made visible. May it be so. Amen.

06 / A Generous Creating

In the Western world, we are always making sense of our faith against the backdrop of global capitalism. The economic vision of a free market with clear losers and winners deeply influences how we talk about God and how we think about art.

When we are doing our making, we must always be mindful of the spirit we are creating from. Are we painting to win? Are we writing to crush? Are we singing to triumph?

Jesus invites us into a generous creating—a creating that does not fear, that is not self-conscious, and that is generative in purpose. That doesn't mean we can't have edges. That we can't say the hard thing. That we can't facilitate a gut check.

But it does mean that ultimately our art should be generous. A gift. A thing given over and over and over because we are called to be love to the whole of the Earth.

Father, search the depths of our souls for the things that crush and destroy and vie to win. Heal the parts of us that long to stand at the top at the expense of others. We confess that we have a long way to go.

Jesus, develop in us a generous living. Help us create from a place of love. Help us make as an act of service. Let our artistic and creative lives reflect your love and sacrifice.

Holy Spirit, give us the humility to be generous. Give us the courage to offer our talents as gifts.

Keep our hearts in check when we are tempted to exert our abilities as a show of power. We need your counsel. Amen.

07 / Collaboration Is a Spiritual Practice

As an extension of our generous creating, we are called to make in community. The context of abundant life is community. In the beginning, God created in community with himself. Father, Son, and Holy Spirit extended generous love and creative potential to each other and into the void to form the universe.

A Trinitarian vision of creating means that as God's image bearers, we, too, are meant to make in community. Collaboration is the artist's way of saying "community." When we collaborate with other people, we are doing something very ancient.

The cultural script that many creatives are given is one of isolation. It is the narrative that you must live alone, you must suffer alone, you must create alone in order to make something meaningful.

We believe in something older, that the creative process of God is baked into the fabric of the cosmos. We are called to do our work of making in collaborative, Trinitarian community. To labor together. To share with each other. To help one another. To love each other. To need one another. To suffer together. As artists, we are sustained by the creative energy of God's community.

Jesus, thank you for being our model of collaboration. Thank you for inviting the disciples to come and be a part of the work that you were doing. Thank you for calling us to be co-creators. We are grateful.

Holy Spirit, keep our hearts open to the new possibilities of collaborative and creative work we might encounter. Draw us into community and bring us into situations where we can create with others.

Father, thank you that your work of creating was done in community. Give us wisdom and discernment as we seek to model our creative endeavors after your example. Amen.

08 / Gratitude Is the Bedrock of Our Remembering

The people of God are called to live lives of remembering the faithfulness of the Lord.

Remembering is what gives us vision for the future.

If we are to remember well, it must begin in our practices of gratitude. As followers of Jesus, and as creatives, we are the recipients of gifts. We use our gifts to be a blessing to the people and community around us. We did not make our gifts (though we may refine them) and we are not our gifts (though we may be told so).

This means that our hearts must continuously be oriented toward gratitude. We are thankful for the ability to make, we are thankful for the freedom to form, we are thankful for the mind we've been given. We are God's handiwork, and that cosmic story is shared in our own making—for this we are grateful.

Gratitude is the bedrock of our remembering. Living in a posture of constant gratitude allows us to approach our work with humility, remembering rightly the God who facilitates our creating.

We are called to create. All we can say is thank you, thank you, thank you, thank you.

Father, thank you. (30-second pause after each)

Jesus, thank you.

Holy Spirit, thank you.

Amen.

09 / Give It All Away

When we decide to follow Jesus, our lives are no longer our own, and our existence gets caught up in the things that God is doing in our time. Our priorities and allegiances shift.

We are filled with the things of God but are called to live lives of sacrificial love. Our lives become abundant in the Spirit, only to be given away.

The reason for cultivating silence, for imagining new realities, for innovating, for creating, for collaborating, and for practicing gratitude is for one thing: so that you can give it all away.

Creatives who follow the way of Jesus are called to give away every last trade secret, every lesson learned, every skill set acquired, and lots and lots of art.

We are blessed to be a blessing.

We are creative, not for ourselves, but for the flourishing of humanity. We start companies, not for personal gain but to reimagine the marketplace as a place of generosity. We make things so that our communities are filled with the creative energy of God, allowing the next generation to join in the work of ushering in shalom.

When creatives build empires and hoard talent, our art becomes propaganda. We are not called to consolidate but to liberate. So give it all away: help those around you start their thing, tell all your artisan secrets, teach the next generation how to create and offer your gift to the world. Give it all away, and see what happens. Amen.

Part Two

On Becoming
Creative

01 / A Theology of Making

When we think about our work of making (our art, our companies, our gardens, our mixtapes, our things in the earth), it is essential that we locate that creative energy deep in our life with God. The call of makers, of those of us who craft, cannot be seen as a separate vocation sprinkled over our knowing Christ but instead as our collective returning to the old things that were true at the foundation of the world.

Where does our creative spark come from? Why does it matter that we make? What is the purpose of our artistic endeavors? How is this relevant to a life with the Lord? These are fundamental and important questions to address when we consider the sacred task of making.

Here are two reflections from the books of Genesis and Exodus. They are meant to be an introduction, an exercise in looking at scripture through the lens of the creative. They are not exhaustive commentaries, but a first step in connecting our making to our life with God. These are launching points for developing a theology of making.

OUR DESIRE TO CREATE
IS AN IMPRINT OF THE DIVINE

The oldest story is one of making. God created. God made. God formed. God took the void and gave it context. And it was good (Gen. 1:1).

It matters that the first action of God was a cosmic, community art project. A triune fellowship, ordering the skies and filling the earth. "In the beginning God created" opens possibility that opens possibility.

We must never forget that creatives are possibility makers. God's vocation as a generous Creator is the first thing before all of the other things in the book of Genesis. This is good news.

As an outflowing of the generous life of God, humans were made (Gen. 1:27). Humanity is a divine design initiative.

If we take seriously that humans are created in God's image, that we are formed as a reflection of our Creator, then the question of how we handle our own particular designing and making becomes vitally important.

God's making fills the Earth with good things. What does this say about how our making ought to be?

Our desire to make finds its energy source in God's divine design initiative. God was the first artist to put something of himself into art, and we have all followed in that legacy. Can we, too, partner with God to fill the earth with good things? Can we, too, launch creative projects that heal, restore, and hope?

The first commandment from God to humans is not found in Exodus, but here in the beginning. "Be fruitful and increase in number"— it is the call to fill the earth and steward it (Gen. 1:28).

Our creating is a part of the unfolding, generative process of God's goodness filling the earth. Our desire to create is an imprint of the divine, designed into the fabric of our existence. Artists and creatives feel this acutely. We are not only invited to create new things (Gen. 2:19) but to partner with God to fill the Earth with the divine creative Spirit that humans received as a gift. Even as a fragmented people, this is still our primary task. It is one of the old things that was true at the foundation of the world, and we cannot afford to forget it.

This does not mean that all the things we make are good, but it does mean that it is good that we are making things. As humans and image reflectors, our invitation is to partner with God in the creative flourishing of creation. We are makers, because God is the First Maker.

CREATIVE PROJECTS CONNECT COMMUNITIES

In the book of Exodus, five chapters (35–40) are devoted to describing the scope of a public work of art, the implementation of its construction, and the impact it has on a community. It is a process shot through with the presence of the Lord. The story begins by describing the Israelites donating a vast array of resources for the public work of the Tabernacle—a moveable construction where the Spirit of the Lord was to dwell (Exod. 35:4–9).

Gold, silver, bronze, various colors of yarn and fine linen, goat hair, ram skins dyed red, durable leather, acacia wood, olive oil, spices, onyx stones, and an assortment of gems are all collected as resources for the Tabernacle project. The things of creation are harvested for a new kind of creating, and everyone from the community is invited to participate in its funding as they are able.

Then comes the invitation to the makers to do their making: "All who are skilled among you are to come and make everything the Lord has commanded" (Exod. 35:10).

Come and make everything the Lord has commanded. Be fruitful and multiply. These are commands coming from the heart of God. The community responds to the call of the Lord and collaborates to make something beautiful in worship to God (Exod. 35:20–29).

Some fund the project and some give their creative skill, but to execute this kind of sacred public work requires the participation of all. Exodus 35 stands at the intersection of generous donation, artisan skill, and divine commandment. The result of that creative labor is a connected community, and one of the singularly important sacred constructions of human history.

The place where the presence of God could dwell among the Israelites was made in a collaborative, sacrificial process (Exod. 40). Each gave what they could in a creative dynamic that allowed the whole of the community to experience the Tabernacle presence of God.

Why does it matter that we make things? Why do we need to bother with creating? Because creative projects connect communities. People to people. People to the earth. And people to God. The common creative spirit placed in all of humanity is a starting point for connection, and even a returning of things fragmented into things made whole again. We are Imago Dei, given the Creator's image, and able to make with one another in the common service of human flourishing.

To rearrange the materials of the earth into something new is to extend possibility into the world. This is our stewardship. It is a part of our fruitfulness and multiplying. And when we do our making together, we are living out our life with God in a full and real way. Our making in community is a part of our returning to the old things that were true at the foundation of the world. And it is good. Amen.

02 / What We Do or Who We Are?

From the beginning, there has been creativity: the story of a God separating sea and earth, animal and man, light and dark. In the Apostles' Creed, God is named as the one who created the heavens and the earth. In Genesis, God is introduced to the reader as a creator.

"In the beginning, God created the heavens and the earth" (Gen. 1:1).

Continuing in Genesis, we see people are also created, and they are done so in the image of God. From the beginning, we are given responsibility and identity in him. We are named as creators, too.

"So God created mankind in his own image, in the image of God he created them; male and female he created them" (Gen. 1:27).

How did we get from creator to creative? The word creator is familiar to our tongues: the maker of something, the one responsible, the origin. Creative is less recognizable—changing—taking on a different meaning in our world today.

We no longer discuss whether or not someone has a creative trait or characteristic, and instead, we wonder if someone has enough of that ability to use it as an identity. But who or what determines whether we are a creative or not? Is it our job title? How much we produce? How often we create? Are we still creative, even when we are not creating?

The changing of creative from a descriptor to an identity misses the mark. It reinforces thinking along the lines of those who "are" and those who "are

not," when in Genesis we see that *all* are creative, all are co-creators, and all are made in the image of a creative God.

Creative was meant to be a way to describe, not define.

Creativity as identity compartmentalizes our being. It simplifies our existence to our production, and divides our life from one another.

We make sense of who we are through the communities that form us.

From our grandmother's malasada recipe and comments that begin with "your generation" to hugging every family member when it's time to go. From hands lifted in protest to hands held in promise, raised in remembrance of waymakers who came before.

We pull together all these threads of stories and experiences to create an identity, knowing that while experiences are momentary, we are who we are when we wake up and when we go to sleep. We remain the same through the beginning to the end, regardless of what happens in the middle.

Nothing changes this—we simply are who we are.

Other identities help us to understand our first identity in Christ. They are acceptable because they are in cohabitation with and submission to the ultimate identity He has given.

Our identities are hidden in Christ, they can't be touched by job changes, results, or in seasons of low production when we feel we have lost our right to call ourselves creative.

Praise God that we may name ourselves as beloved, as co-creators, as image bearers regardless of appearance or result. The truth is, these divine definitions of who we are run so deep that they are tattooed to both an unchanging reality and a future of hope. It is only a matter of time before we become who Christ says we already are.

03 / A Lesson in Beginning

Making art is almost certainly an act of courage and bravery.

To make something, and put a piece of yourself into that thing, is no small feat. We mimic our Creator and make things that reflect our lives. This is called love, but it is very hard to do.

When we talk about the barriers, the things that keep us from pursuing art, we are also talking about what it means to be brave. Alongside our bravery, we must also consider humility. Creating meaningful art requires a humility about our lives, our work, and our process. If we lack humility, the process of beginning again and again and again will overwhelm us, and we'll walk away from our creative calling for something that doesn't cost so much.

This may be why Jesus tells his disciples that, "unless a kernel of wheat falls to the ground and dies, it remains only a single seed. But if it dies, it produces many seeds." (John 12:24)

We must have courage to face that kind of dying, and in that death, embrace a limitless kind of living. There are the seeds of many creative dreams inside of us, if only we have the humility to let them emerge.

As we consider the barriers that all creatives must face in some form or another, here are three that are valuable to name and reflections on how they might be overcome.

I NEED TO BE PERFECT

There's a lot to be said about the pressures that we put on ourselves as humans. We often think that we need to become God in order for anything good or worthwhile to happen in our lives.

For the artist, this looks like self-obsessed living and the kind of devotion to craft that destroys relationships. It is a fine thing to be dedicated to improving but another thing to think that this dedication will save us from suffering.

We are imperfect people, brought forward by Christ into God's loving presence. From this place we do our making, our creating, and our innovating.

IT NEEDS TO BE PERFECT

Sometimes it's just time to ship it, be done and move on. We are actually stifling creative flow when we forever come back to the same project over and over and over again. We cannot begin again and again and again if we never finish our projects, plays, or poems.

Nothing we make should happen in the pursuit of perfection. A bunch of honest, creative messes are better than the endless refinement of one thing that you never share with the world.

THE MESSAGE NEEDS TO BE PERFECT

A significant barrier for emerging creatives is the tendency to try to force a message into the medium in which

they find themselves working. To paraphrase poet Richard Hugo, a poem titled "Autumn Rain" better not be about autumn rain.2

When we decide on a message and try to reverse engineer our art around that core message, we lose something important from the creative process. This is the opposite of a generative approach to our making.

God's model is one of openness. When Adam is invited to name the animals, there is possibility. Real creative options exist. God doesn't tell Adam to create around a core set of principles. Instead, the Lord, "brought them to the man to see what he would name them; and whatever the man called each living creature, that was its name" (Gen. 2).

In the Genesis 2 vision of creating, there is openness. True things happen in the process, but truth is not coerced.

Our art will almost certainly say true things, but when we try to force a message, we cease to make art and end up with propaganda.

Our messaging will be messy because we are messy. It is a fine thing to say

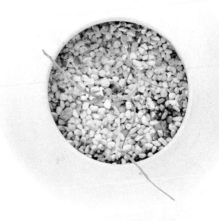

that "love your neighbor" is your launching point, but when we feel bound to always bring our creative project back to that topic, we are stifling the possibility of new things within us. Let things unfold, and let them be what they become.

PRACTICING ART, PRACTICING RESURRECTION

Making art is an act of bravery. There are no guaranteed outcomes and we don't know how any of this will actually shake out. We don't get to control the barriers, only whether or not we will face them. Or, like Charles Bukowski wrote, "What matters most is how well you walk through the fire."3

When we consider the moment we choose to face our barriers, it may be good to remember the bravest thing that Bilbo Baggins ever did in J. R. R. Tolkien's novel, *The Hobbit*:

"A sound, too, began to throb in his ears, a sort of bubbling like the noise of a large pot galloping on the fire, mixed with a rumble as of a gigantic tom-cat purring. This grew to the unmistakable gurgling noise of some vast animal snoring in its sleep down there in the red glow in front of him."

"It was at this point that Bilbo stopped. Going on from there was the bravest thing he ever did. The tremendous things that happened afterwards were as nothing compared to it. He fought the real battle in the tunnel alone, before he ever saw the vast danger that lay in wait."4

The hardest part is walking toward the things that will seemingly result in our death. It isn't the struggle, it isn't the battle, and it isn't the making. It is the moment when we clearly see all the ways we could be crushed by continuing and still take a step forward. In our pursuit of art, we learn the courage to face death, failure, and fear. It is the bravery of walking toward the things that feel impossible. It is the knowing that to practice our art is to practice resurrection again and again and again. Amen.

04 / Creativity as Devotional Practice

Somewhere along the way, creativity becomes a means to an end.

It's not a hobby anymore; it's a career. It's not an activity; it's activism. It's not playtime; it's productivity. It's not for leisure; it's our legacy.

In a society where artists are idolized and then monetized, creativity is a valuable commodity.

It's no wonder we experience burnout. We are frustrated when we fail to meet our goals. Disappointed when our work goes unrecognized. Afraid when it doesn't pay the bills.

We are left spent and tired and wondering why we create at all. There's enough noise in the world. Why are we adding to it?

In those moments, it helps to think about the ending and the beginning.

The Ending: What if you quit? Or rather, what keeps you from quitting? The Beginning: Why did you start creating in the first place?

These two questions remind us of the curious energy that sprang out of us when we were young, and of the quiet urge that never fails to return even when we vow to silence it forever. Creativity always begins as an involuntary response to the world around us.

As creativity becomes intertwined with our identity and livelihood, we forget its intrinsic value. We think everything must have a practical purpose—but isn't life more than a series of accomplishments?

We've forgotten that pleasure isn't sinful, and so we scramble for ways to justify that which brings us joy.

When we start seeing art as a means to an end, we forget that it was often small, childlike moments that led us to God's presence. When we approach creativity as a devotional practice, experiencing God's presence is placed at the center of our process. To borrow the words of the Westminster Shorter Catechism, "Our chief end becomes to glorify God and to enjoy him."5

God wanted to walk with us in the Garden in the cool of the day. He wanted to watch us name the animals. He wanted to enjoy us, and for us to enjoy him. When we create, we are fully present to God's presence. It calls us back to the childlike contentment of spending time with a parent or loved one.

By laying down our burden of needing to be needed and surrendering our longing for significance, we strike down the lie that we must somehow earn our privilege to exist. We declare that any activity with God is sacred, no matter how frivolous it may seem to the outside world. And we are free to enjoy the simple act of creation because we know that every good and perfect gift comes from God.

Many of our stories began in the secrecy of our bedrooms, strumming an instrument or writing in the pages of our journal. For others, it was the meditative practice of exploring the world through a clear glass lens or painting with our fingers.

These quiet moments gave us a glimpse of the divine, a gut feeling that God was sharing our space. Or maybe creativity felt like a wrestling match with God— more an argument than a conversation—or even a tense confrontation with ourselves. Either way, as we engaged with him, we were changed.

We place enormous amounts of pressure on ourselves to be world-changing or to make art "productive," but we can only really do what God has created us to do: spend time in his presence.

Rather than burdening ourselves with yet another expectation, let us instead view creativity as a devotional practice for reconnecting with our first love. May it be so.

05 / The Creative Process Is Fueled by 1,000 Failures

Here is the hard thing: the creative process is inextricably linked to the experience of failure, criticism, and even death. This is not easy, and it is not fun, but it is essential to name and address. As Christians, we are a people who believe that when things are destroyed, newness is possible. But sometimes failure just feels like failure. Somehow, the cross provides a way for death to become new life. Living into this reality is the ongoing struggle of our lives.

So when we imagine and plan for our life of making, innovating, and creating, we must also expect the death that comes with it. Our poem may die in the third round of edits, our album might never get the producer it needs, and our painting might just not get there regardless of what we add or take away. This is hard for us, but it is something we must face.

To paraphrase Anne Lamott, there are a good number of us who happen to believe that if we do everything *just right*, we won't have to experience death.6 But the creative process is fueled by death, failure, and critique. They are the millions of small things that engender humility, gratitude, and perseverance in our art. They are the reality of the cross in our making. And they are necessary.

Art is a kind of continual dying, but that death always leads the way into something new. This is the great mystery.

ON MENTORSHIP, CRITICISM, AND FRIENDSHIP

In this journey towards new-life-through-death, we need guides to point us toward resurrection. They might appear as moments, or relationships that last for our whole lives. These experiences are fluid but essential for creatives to lean into.

The three guiding experiences of the creative life are mentorship, criticism,

and friendship. People will embody these experiences at different points in their lives. If we let them, they can become powerful guides that can catalyze us through the things that feel like death and into a creating that looks like new life.

Mentorship

Mentorship is the antidote to failure. We all need the experience of mentorship. People who are farther down the road, who can give perspective, advice, and encouragement, are a practical cornerstone of deep living. We need elders, experts, and leaders who can look through our wounds and see the potential for newness that exists on the other side. Often, mentors are the ones who can hold the fragments of our dream and show us how the pieces might begin to fit back together.

Criticism

It is easy to avoid criticism of our art, but it means never sharing anything with the world. If we are to make art that matters, opening ourselves up to criticism is an important rhythm. We need people who will push against our assumptions and call us to great-

er skill. It is a gift to lean into critique because art is always a dialogue between the creator and the community. And sometimes the critics are right. Sometimes we do need to get better. Sometimes the creative thing we've been pushing for isn't the right thing. We can be wrong. These voices can be valuable if we put them in their right place: directed at our art and not at our identity.

Friendship

Creative friends and partners are a blessing. They walk with us through the birth of our ideas and become the hospice workers to our dreams when things do not work out as we hoped. Creative friendship is a sacred thing, and is often what helps us weather the things that feel like death. Friends like these are full of hope but will not withhold the truth. They share in our process, and each person grows from the generative thing at the center of their knowing one another. Friendship is the place where our wounds and failures are held in the hands of another. Friendship is the mysterious union that allows us to hope for the new life on the other side of our present dying.

06 / When You Get There, Remember That You Were Carried by the Spirit

One day you will arrive at the place where making things becomes a sustained part of your life. You will craft, master, and refine your skills. Your creativity will become integrated into the rhythms of living that make up the content of your days on this earth.

You will *arrive*. And when you arrive, you will need to decide what story you will tell about how you got there.

As creatives, it is essential that we have an honest relationship with ourselves about how we've come to the place that we are. That we remember what carried us forward when our making things felt impossible or stupid or like a bad idea. We have teachers, friends, family, landscapes, and failures that helped refine our spirit, and it's essential that these things are named, held close, and honored.

Our creating is a product of all of our life. We live integrated existences of soul and blood and music and wonder and ink and earth and dreams and stars and words and history. We must become creative people who remember the things that carried us forward.

It is not unlike the life of Samuel, whose memory of the things in the past informed his leadership of the people of God into the future. Samuel remembered God and God's faithfulness to his people.

"Then Samuel took a stone and set it up between Mizpah and Shen. He named it Ebenezer, saying, 'Thus far the Lord has helped us.'" (1 Samuel 7:12)

We are called to lay ebenezers along the road of our creative journey. Our memory of God's work in our lives,

and the people that facilitated it, must be at the foundation of our creative imagination. We must remember what carried us.

Each artistic project we undertake is an ebenezer to specific moments in our lives. These stones become the foundation of our creative ecology, and they are immeasurably valuable instruments of memory and worship.

A clear sense of memory about God's active work and generosity in our lives allows us to live lives of hospitality. We can welcome, embrace, and share freely because we know that we are not singularly responsible for creative energy pulsing through our bodies and into the world. It has been cultivated, grown, and tended to by the communities we call home and by the God who holds all things together in himself. As creatives, we are always being held in the hospitality of another Creator.

REMEMBER

One day you will arrive, and when you arrive you will need to decide what story you will tell about how you got there.

The temptation will be to add another story to the cannon of creation myths that place us at the center. The things college dropouts start in their parent's garage. The broken hearts that forever tell truth. The rebel that burns all their bridges on the road to changing reality. The sadness, the anger, the hurt, and the beauty.

These stories of our perseverance, hustle, and grit eliminate the role that others play in our developing creative imagination. God becomes a passive bystander to our brilliance.

Entrepreneurship and memory conflict, and in those moments, we must return to the stones of our remembrance. We were carried by the Spirit. This is the story we tell again and again and again. The stone we work back and forth in the palm of our hand. The song we sing when we walk around our neighborhood at the end of the day.

One day, you will arrive. And when you get there, remember that you were carried by Spirit. Hallelujah. Amen. May it be so.

Part Three

Creativity in the Life of Jesus

01 / The Creative Energy of Baptism and Wilderness

"At that time Jesus came from Nazareth in Galilee and was baptized by John in the Jordan. Just as Jesus was coming up out of the water, he saw heaven being torn open and the Spirit descending on him like a dove. And a voice came from heaven: 'You are my Son, whom I love; with you I am well pleased.'"

"At once the Spirit sent him out into the wilderness, and he was in the wilderness forty days, being tempted by Satan. He was with the wild animals, and angels attended him." (Mark 1:9–13)

...

The banks of the Jordan. The river. The life that is submerged and the life that rises up and into the world. This is how it begins: heaven torn open, and the Spirit of God flowing down into creation. The world is a story of things that unfold.

Before Jesus had done anything of importance, substance, or value, he was affirmed as a son, who is loved, and whose existence is pleasing to God. Nothing proved, nothing earned, only a state of belovedness tied solely to his existing in the world. To exist is to be loved by God.

As creatives, it is essential that we consider the things that were true before we ever made anything. God's love for us is first. To be made in God's image, to be a child of God, is not a status we achieve but a thing that is true forever.

Before our making, we are invited to consider how we are made, how we are loved, and how we are held closely in the presence of God.

Our creating flows out of our *baptism*. The things that have died, the things that are transformed, the things that are being birthed.

Immediately after his baptism, the Spirit drives Jesus out into the wilderness. It reveals a fundamental truth about this life: that baptism and wilderness are always interlocked. New life and the space that refines it are connected at a cosmic level.

When our creating flows out of baptism, we are able to engage with the wilderness.

Our new life and suffering are always holding hands. In Jesus's life, baptism leads to wilderness. As creatives, it is important that we not miss the connection between new energy and deep challenge. That our excitement, love, and hope about the future is connected to the pain, suffering, and sorrow of the wilderness.

In the life of Jesus, we see God's great unfolding toward life. It is this first love that carries Jesus through the wilderness, and it is the same first love that we must hold fast to in our daily living.

02 / Who Is This For?

"Once again Jesus went out beside the lake. A large crowd came to him, and he began to teach them. As he walked along, he saw Levi son of Alphaeus sitting at the tax collector's booth. 'Follow me,' Jesus told him, and Levi got up and followed him."

"While Jesus was having dinner at Levi's house, many tax collectors and sinners were eating with him and his disciples, for there were many who followed him. When the teachers of the law who were Pharisees saw him eating with the sinners and tax collectors, they asked his disciples: 'Why does he eat with tax collectors and sinners?'"

"On hearing this, Jesus said to them, 'It is not the healthy who need a doctor, but the sick. I have not come to call the righteous, but sinners.'" (Mark 2:13–17)

...

In this story, Jesus is challenging the assumptions of the religious leaders of his time. In his interactions with Levi, Jesus takes a traitor to his people (re: tax collector) and brings him back into relationship with the community. Levi's identity is transformed from economic oppressor to generous host.

Jesus models a way of living that has space for those on the outside and on the margins of the community. It is offensive to religious leaders, and it is good news.

This radical hospitality for those on the outside brings up a fundamental question about the life and ministry of Jesus: "Who is this for?"

For creatives, this is a fundamental question that we must address when considering our making.

Who is our art for?
What table are we setting?
Who is invited?
Who have we excluded?
Does it heal?
Is it generous?

The life of Jesus was not life for life's sake. It had a purpose, a rhythm, and a direction. It was for those in search of healing. The life of Jesus was a life for others.

When we consider the creative task, it is essential that we honor the question, "Who is this for?", and then seek to answer it with the kind of hospitality modeled for us in the life of Jesus.

Our creative endeavors must give shape to good news. When assessing the "goodness" of our art, we must look to the embodied living of Jesus and let that life open up a different vision of what makes creative things valuable. Does it bring a healing word? Can it carry people through suffering? Will it leave us in awe of the things around us? Does it transform? Did it bring us into a moment of presence?

In the creative life, hospitality is the only metric that matters.

03 / The Mysterious Things That Happen in the Dirt

"He also said, 'This is what the kingdom of God is like. A man scatters seed on the ground. Night and day, whether he sleeps or gets up, the seed sprouts and grows, though he does not know how. All by itself the soil produces grain—first the stalk, then the head, then the full kernel in the head. As soon as the grain is ripe, he puts the sickle to it, because the harvest has come.'"

"Again he said, 'What shall we say the kingdom of God is like, or what parable shall we use to describe it? It is like a mustard seed, which is the smallest of all seeds on earth. Yet when planted, it grows and becomes the largest of all garden plants, with such big branches that the birds can perch in its shade.'" (Mark 4:26–32)

...

When Jesus teaches, he commonly makes use of parables to illustrate complex concepts in concise ways. These stories are rooted in images, experiences, and environmental realities that his audience would have understood.

Parables are an exercise in possibility. It is language used to explode our thinking about God, people, and how the Spirit works in the world to accomplish good.

Jesus makes use of agrarian images to get his audience into deeper thinking about the working nature of the Kingdom of God. They are earthy images for a generative world. God's rule is in the small, buried things that one day will emerge in the glory of new life, with hues of green that look like salvation.

As creatives, we must learn to integrate the workings of the Kingdom into our own creative processes.

The Kingdom of God is the small thing that grows beyond what was expected.

Its impact is exponential but mysterious. We don't get to control it. We don't know exactly how it all turns out. We just know that it is happening.

Our art is not so different.

We make, craft, create, curate, and design. And then we let it go.

The seed is planted in the world, and we do not get to decide whether it lives or dies.

We do not get to control or know the impact of what we offer to others. What we've made is no longer ours. It is in the world.

We do not know who might find shelter in the things that we have made. We should see this as a liberating reality. It allows us to approach our craft with humility. We are serving people we do not know. This is a sacred task.

We are invited to faithfully make and trust that the mysterious things that happen in the dirt will be enough.

A plant doesn't control who enjoys its fruit. A tree doesn't know who will find shelter in its branches. An artist never really knows who will be saved by what they have made. This is the Divine mystery of the creative process.

04 / Divine Weirdness and the Creative Life

"They came to Bethsaida, and some people brought a blind man and begged Jesus to touch him. He took the blind man by the hand and led him outside the village. When he had spit on the man's eyes and put his hands on him, Jesus asked, 'Do you see anything?'"

"He looked up and said, 'I see people; they look like trees walking around.'"

"Once more Jesus put his hands on the man's eyes. Then his eyes were opened, his sight was restored, and he saw everything clearly." (Mark 8:22–25)

...

As we reflect on the life of Jesus and consider what that life means for those of us who create, it is important that we pay attention to the things that give us pause.

The weirdness of Jesus is a powerful thing.

This strange story revolves around Jesus, a blind man, spit, and the shape that healing takes in a person's life.

Like many of Jesus's healing stories, there are things happening on multiple levels.

On one level, this is Jesus bringing tangible healing to a man desperate for relief. This is the raw, embodied, physical divinity of Jesus' life.

On another level, the conditions of this man's life mirror the conditions of the Jewish religious leaders that Jesus interacts with: blind, or at best, seeing it partly.

The restoration that Jesus enacts in this story is both immediately real and cosmically symbolic.

Jesus brings restoration in a way that feels like an outsider art experience. Spit, bodies, spoken word, and sequential experiences. The weirdness of this healing is art.

Divine weirdness is an essential element of the creative life.

It's the weird things that wake us up to the world around us.

It's the weird things that open up new ways of seeing.

It's the weird things that reimagine the experience of healing.

It's the weird things that disrupt our lives to bring us into God's presence.

It's the weird things that show us people like trees.

Weirdness is a tool of the Divine. As people of faith, our lives get weird before they become clear.

The task of the creative is to use the weird things of creation in the service of the Creator. To serve the people who see in part, and help them see "everything clearly." Worthwhile art disrupts in the service of restoration.

05 / Seeing Beyond Seeing

"Jesus sat down opposite the place where the offerings were put and watched the crowd putting their money into the temple treasury. Many rich people threw in large amounts. But a poor widow came and put in two very small copper coins, worth only a few cents."

"Calling his disciples to him, Jesus said, 'Truly I tell you, this poor widow has put more into the treasury than all the others. They all gave out of their wealth; but she, out of her poverty, put in everything—all she had to live on.'" (Mark 12:41–44)

...

There is art that is not made but observed in real life. It is seeing a thing that happens in the world from an alternative perspective that opens up truth. There are moments in the gospels where Jesus teaches not through original content but by reflecting what is actually happening in the world, illustrating truth about the nature of God.

Jesus models a seeing that is beyond seeing. While his disciples see the mass of people giving offerings, Jesus articulates the nuance of the moment. There was a worship beneath the worship. Giving beyond giving. It is an elemental teaching, something we know deep in our souls: that two people doing the same action are not bound to the same motivation, nor are they guaranteed the same experience.

It is important to note the way that Jesus teaches the disciples in this passage.

The prophetic word that Jesus brought was embedded in a living experience. The lesson taught was not a hypothetical, but a real moment that people watched unfold.

Truth was embodied in a real moment in space and time. Something happened, and because of where Jesus was standing, we're still talking about it now. It is an observation that has echoed across 2,000 years of life.

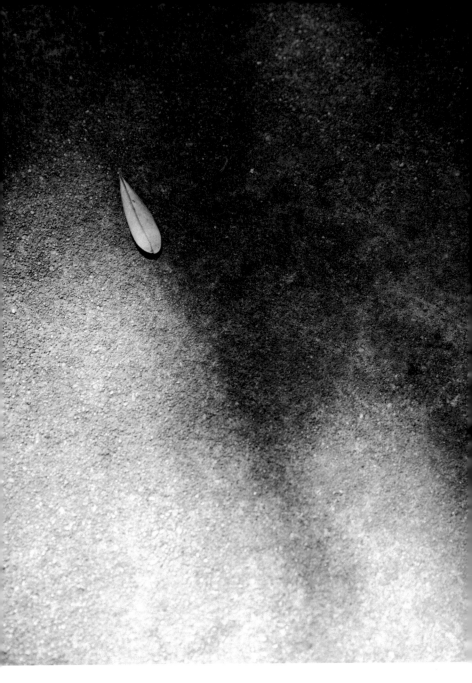

Creative, holy teaching is often a matter of seeing.

Jesus's teaching itself also brings an important perspective to the creative experience. When we offer our creative gift from a place of poverty, we are getting closer to the kind of spiritual exchange that God honors. In the liminal space, when we are stretched to our limits, we find transformation.

Creativity out of poverty levels the playing field. Making out of all that we lack actually means that all are able to be a part of God's working in the world.

The ability to offer our gifts in worship to God and service to others is not a special privilege reserved for skilled artisans. When we show up, and when we offer what we have, we are giving ourselves over to the mystery.

Somehow, this is worship.
Somehow, God sees it.
Somehow, God honors it.
Somehow.

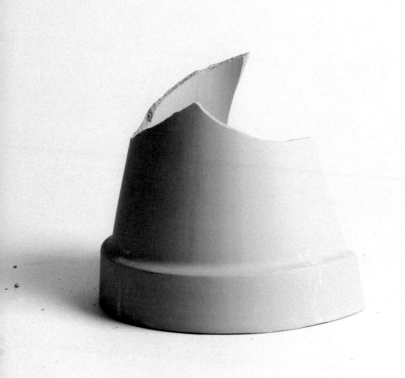

06 / Epilogue

"At noon, darkness came over the whole land until three in the afternoon. And at three in the afternoon Jesus cried out in a loud voice, 'Eloi, Eloi, lema sabachthani?' (which means 'My God, my God, why have you forsaken me?')."

"When some of those standing near heard this, they said, 'Listen, he's calling Elijah.'"

"Someone ran, filled a sponge with wine vinegar, put it on a staff, and offered it to Jesus to drink. 'Now leave him alone. Let's see if Elijah comes to take him down,' he said."

"With a loud cry, Jesus breathed his last."

"The curtain of the temple was torn in two from top to bottom. And when the centurion, who stood there in front of Jesus, saw how he died, he said, 'Surely this man was the Son of God!'" (Mark 15:33–39)

"Art must die and be reborn in everything" – Vladimir Tatlin

In the gospel of Mark, Jesus dies a brutal death. His life does not end with words of forgiveness, but with doubt and a loud cry. It is a jarring thing to read, and not how we typically think of Jesus on the cross.

Often, our popular images of Jesus suffering are created with an eye toward triumph.

It's almost as if the suffering of Jesus wasn't real but an illusion that a divine being orchestrated to prove a larger cosmic point.

Here's the thing: Jesus died a physical death. He suffered. His incarnation was full, and because he was fully present to the human experience, it was real. Jesus on the cross is not a spiritual exercise. It is blood, pain, and suffering. What, then, is there for us to learn about the creative life in Jesus on the cross? How do we approach the focal point of human history without trivializing it?

The cross is where the lines between sacrificial living and the creative process

get blurred. The cross is what liberates artists to become a people for others. The cross is the way things that are death become life. The cross is the cosmic dismantling of tools that destroy in the service of life universal.

The cross is for everyone—and everything—everywhere.

In Jesus's death, and eventually in his resurrection, we are invited to see beyond seeing. We die so that others might experience life. This is the life of Jesus, this is the life of the Christian, and this is the life of the creative. A life for others. That is the current that runs throughout the course of the life of Jesus.

Creatives are called to be people for others. This is the reverberation of God's love in our lives. Our art, our making, our creating, and our dreaming is always to be in the service of others. Creativity that looks like the life of Jesus also looks like his death: sacrificial, vulnerable, and, mysteriously, for others.

 ALABASTER

EDITOR-IN-CHIEF | HEAD OF WRITING
Geoff Gentry

CO-FOUNDER | CREATIVE DIRECTOR
Bryan Ye-Chung

CO-FOUNDER | BUSINESS DIRECTOR
Brian Chung

WORDS
Geoff Gentry
Adrian Patenaude
Alana Freitas
Evie Shaffer

IMAGES
Jacob Chung
Echo Yun Chen
Kristen S. Hahn
Jonathan Martin
Bryan Ye-Chung

OPERATIONS DIRECTOR
Willa Jin

GRAPHIC DESIGNER
Tyler Zak

SOCIAL MEDIA DIRECTOR
Kay Xie

ENDNOTES

1. Kahlil Gibran, "On Work," in The Prophet (Alfred A. Knopf, 1923.)

2. Richard Hugo, "Writing Off the Subject," in The Triggering Town: Lectures and Essays on Poetry and Writing (W.W. Norton, 2010).

3. Charles Bukowski, What Matters Most Is How Well You Walk Through the Fire (Ecco/HarperCollins Pub., 2002).

4. J. R. R. Tolkien, The Hobbit, or, There and Back Again (Houghton Mifflin Harcourt, 2012).

5. The Westminster Shorter Catechism (Board of Christian Education of the Presbyterian Church in the U.S.A., 1936).

6. Anne Lamott, "Perfectionism," in Bird by Bird (Anchor Books, 1997).